Dedication

To the Only Wise God, for using me in this endeavor.

To my loving, supportive wife Monica and our children, Elizabeth, James, Ann Marie and Michael, without whose unselfish sacrifice this book would never have come to be.

Io my mother and father (Mr. & Mrs. Prince O. Teal), upon whose shoulders I stand as I reach toward my tomorrow.

To Rev. Dr. P. L. Barrett, who taught me by example that thorough study of the Word is the duty of every Christian.

To Rev. E. A. Heyliger, Min. Daisy Clark and the Ferguson Memorial Baptist Church family, for recognizing and stirring up The Gift in me.

To Rev. Dr. Carl Bentley, for encouraging me to publish this work and for taking the time to help me edit it.

To April Washington and Threefold Music Group for sowing a wonderful seed into the ministry that God has given me by giving me a chance to share this word from The Word with the Body.

To my friend, co-worker and Godmother, Pastor Betty Steele, for helping shape me and this book through her "on-the-job" ministry.

To Rev. Dr. Linda H. Hollies for helping me to understand the liberating import of Galations 3:28 and for teaching me to edit, edit, edit.

To the Webminister (R. McCollum), Will, Rev. Fullard, Gina, McCottry, Wayne, Ron B., Hammondfan, Destiny, Sharyelj, Rev. Phillips, Dewayne, Ms. Gwen, Shelton and the rest of the crew at www.blackgospel.com's discussion board for helping to shape this work.

1st edition/1st printing published September 22, 1999 by Rodney A. Teal
2nd edition/1st printing revised October 9,1999 by Rodney A. Teal
2nd edition/2nd printing revised January 7, 2000 by Rodney A. Teal
3rd edition/1st printing revised March 2000 by Rodney A. Teal
3rd edition/2nd printing published October 2000 by Rodney A. Teal
3rd edition/3rd printing published April 2001 by Rodney A. Teal
4th edition/1st printing published August 2001 by Rodney A. Teal
4th edition/2nd printing published January 2002 by Rodney A. Teal
4th edition/3rd printing published April 2002 by Rodney A. Teal
4th edition/4th printing published May 2003 by Rodney A. Teal
5th edition/1st printing published August 2003 by Rodney A. Teal
5th edition/2nd printing published March 2004 by Rodney A. Teal
5th edition/3rd printing published August 2004 by Rodney A. Teal
5th edition/4th printing published December 2004 by Rodney A. Teal
6th edition/1st printing published April 2005

ISBN: **0-615-11304-4**

D1475191

Author's Foreword

Praise & worship . . . Is it one thing or two? Is there a difference between "praise" and "worship"? How are "praise" and/or "worship" different from *praise & worship*? Is "praise" more important than "worship"? Is "worship" more important than "praise"? Must one follow the other? Can you have one without the other? How is music related to these concepts? These are some of the issues that I hope to cover in the material that follows.

In studying this material, keep a Bible handy. We will be looking at "praise," "worship" and "praise & worship" from a BIBLICAL perspective, examining these and related concepts in the Light of God's Word. I hope that as the Spirit of God leads us into this journey, you will be able to answer all of the questions posited in the first paragraph and come to a better understanding of the phenomenon we call "praise & worship." "Praise and worship" is not a destination. It is a journey that we must learn to make as we commune with God and allow God to commune with us.

If I had to pick one theme that I want to share with the Body of Christ through this work, it would be this: "Be an *act-er* not a *feel-er* because neither 'praise' nor 'worship' are emotions. They are verbs." How we feel is irrelevant. We praise because God commands it. We worship because we acknowledge God's "worthy-ship."

May God bless you in your study as I have been blessed in this preparation.

Rev. Rodney A. Teal
www.revrodneyteal.org

LET THERE BE PRAISE AND WORSHIP!!!

Table of Contents

I. Background: Definitions, Concepts and Constructs....................7
   Praise..7
   How Do We Praise?...8
   What Is Worship?...9
   The Relationship Between Worship & Sacrifice...................12
   Comparing/Contrasting *Praise* and *Worship*.......................13

II. *Corporate* Praise & Worship...19
   The "Cloud Experience": Paradigm & Pitfall....................19
   Singing Soldiers: The Battle Is Not Yours...........................22
   Praising Prisoners: Morning at Midnight...........................24
   More Than A Song: Praying for Peter...............................25

III. *Individual* Praise & Worship...27
   Worship By A Sinner: Luke 7:36-50...................................28
   More On Individual Worship...32
      a. Worship Through Following: Matthew 4:18-22........33
      b. Worship Through Giving: I Kings 17: 8-16..............34

IV. Leading Corporate Praise & Worship..................................37
   "Ministry"..37
   The "Call" to Ministry 37
   Being A Leader 39
   The Prophetic Nature of Music Ministry.............................40
   The Role of Instrumental Music in Praise and Worship 41

V. Concluding Thoughts...43

VI. Epilogue: "Triple Point"..45

VII. Sheet Music..55
   Praise..57
   A Song of Thanks..58
   You Are God...59
   Why My Praise..60
   Lord, You Are Great..61

Reflections on Praise & Worship
from a Biblical Perspective

The hardest part of addressing this complex subject is deciding where to begin. In order to get us on the "same page," as it were, let us begin with a brief background, where we examine some basic definitions, discuss related concepts and explore some constructs that will buoy our study . . .

I. Background: Definitions, Concepts and Constructs

Praise

Praise means "to commend; to express approval or admiration; to extol in word or song or deed." It is the way in which one demonstrates, through activity that is readily observable by third-parties, one's thankfulness to God. Praise may be "direct" or "indirect."

Direct praise occurs when one commends, expresses approval or admiration, or extols God to God. The Bible says we should do this "continually." See Hebrews 13:15. Indirect praise occurs when one commends, expresses approval or admiration, or extols God in the presence of others.

Indirect praise is a by-product of direct praise and may be termed witness. Allow me to clarify. Because God is omniscient and omnipresent, we can't praise God without Him being aware of it. In other words, there can be no indirect praise, unless there is direct praise. Thus, when we speak of indirect praise, we use the word "indirect" as a descriptor of the word "praise" from the vantage of those ("eavesdroppers") who witness our witness.

Let's explore the concept of witness further. We may witness "intentionally" or "unintentionally." For example, we may intentionally witness to someone by telling them about God's goodness. This is our responsibility as Christians. See The Great Commission (Matthew 28:19). We may also intentionally witness by lifting our hands (or shouting unto the Lord, etc.) in front of and for the purpose of showing others that we are grateful to God.

Further, we may give an <u>unintentional witness</u> by our demeanor, our speech, our lifestyle, etc. This "unintentional, indirect praise" is our <u>walk</u>. We are, after all, God's ambassadors in all that we do. II Corinthians 5:20. We are charged with the responsibility to invite others to become "reconciled to God." How can we do that effectively when our walk does not demonstrate that have drawn water from the wells of salvation and have done so with joy? *See* Isaiah 12:3.

<u>How Do We Praise?</u>

In Providential Wisdom and for Divine purposes, God has ordained that praise be demonstrative. Praise is always visible and/or audible. It must be expressed physically. You may have a thankful heart (which is where praise and worship must begin), but unless you give expression to the thanksgiving in your heart, you have not praised God.

"But," you say, "God knows my heart. All that noise and all those gyrations aren't necessary. It doesn't take all of that. I'm praising God in my own way." WRONG!

God's Word tells us how to praise God. God expects us to follow Biblical instruction.

Praise is an offering that is tendered by the praiser to God. Psalms 27:6; Amos 5:23. Leviticus 10 reminds us of the danger of rendering an unauthorized offering. God sees it as "strange fire" and will not honor it. Two of Aaron's sons offered "strange fire" to the Lord and paid for it with their lives. Leviticus 10:2. How many spiritual casualties have been suffered in the body of Christ for this same reason?

The Bible is a veritable "praise manual." Here is the top-ten list, with selected (but by no means exhaustive) scriptural references:

1. *clapping hands*- Psalms 47:1
2. *dancing*- Exodus 15:20-21; Psalms 30:11; Acts 3:8
3. *kneeling*- Psalms 95:6

4. *lifting hands*- Psalms 28:2; Timothy 2:8
5. *playing musical instruments*- Psalms 150
6. *prostration*- Revelation 19:4
7. *shouting*-Psalms 47:1 (also, "Make a joyful noise . . . " can be more literally translated "Shout for joy . . . "; see Psalms 66:1)
8. *singing*- the entire book of Psalms
9. *standing*- Psalms 135:2; Revelation 4:9-11
10. *testifying*- Psalms 26:7; Psalms 22:22

Any one of these methods can be used to praise God— to publish the thankfulness that is in our heart. *See, e.g.,* Psalms 66:8. All of these praises have this in common: they require overt action on the part of the praiser.

Still not convinced that praise must be visible and/or audible? Remember Jesus' ride into Jerusalem on that first Palm Sunday? The Bible says in Luke 19:37: "the whole multitude of the disciples began to rejoice and praise God with a loud voice for all the mighty works that they had seen." The Bible further relates that the Pharisees got upset about all the commotion. Jesus told them this: "...if these should hold their peace, the stones would immediately cry out." (v. 40) As the Psalmist says, we are to make the voice of His praise to be heard. Psalms 66:8.

God rightfully demands praise. Psalms 150. The Bible tells us how to praise God. We are free to choose the method of praise that we will use, but we must choose among the alternatives that God has given. You can't praise God "your own way." And you can't praise God anybody else's way, for that matter. You must praise God God's Way.

What Is Worship?

Before we begin, let's make it clear that "worship" eludes precise definition. In truth, "worship" must be experienced. For purposes of our discussion, I have chosen a comprehensive definition that is loosely based on one of a list of definitions posited by Bob Sorge in *Exploring Worship* (1987). I have modified the language in light of my personal experience and Bible study, as well as several sermons that I have heard over the years. I am particularly fond of this definition because it highlights both the sacrificial and the intimately personal nature of the phenomenon we call "worship" and because it clearly demonstrates that Man's purpose is discovered, reclaimed and fulfilled through worship. All this having been said, here is our working definition:

> Worship - *an act by a redeemed man or woman (the creature) toward God (the Creator) whereby his/her will, intellect and emotions gratefully respond in reverence, honor and devotion to the continuing revelation by God of God's Person and Will.*

This definition highlights several important aspects about the experience we call "worship." Let's look at some of them:

1. Worship is a deliberate act directed to God.

We are able to choose to worship or to choose not to do so. The response is ours to make. As God reveals The Divine Self and The Divine Will to us, we can choose to acknowledge God or not.

2. Worship is the grateful surrender of "self" (will, intellect and emotions).

The "will" directs our actions. The "will" is influenced by the "intellect" (i.e., what we comprehend through cognitive processes) and the "emotions" (i.e., what we feel). Let's make our working definition of "worship" a little less theoretical. Read Genesis 3.

It was Man's will, as influenced by his and her intellect and emotions, that led to Man's demise in the garden of Eden. The bottom line is this: Man made the conscious decision (i.e., "willed") to disobey God's command. Man's intellect told him and her that the serpent's reasoning was correct. Man's emotions told him and her that the fruit of the Tree of the Knowledge of Good and Evil was "pleasing to the eye" and "good for food."

You might say that Man fell when he and she stopped worshiping God— when Man exalted him/her "self" above God's "Self." Worship simply puts us back where we started— in tune with God, in fellowship with The Divine! Through worship, we discover, reclaim and fulfill our Divine Purpose!

Our intellect tells us what we "ought" to do, in the normative sense. But our intellect is limited. We don't know everything. When we surrender our "intellect" in worship, we acknowledge that God is omniscient. An important element of worship is to rely on God's knowledge. Even when God asks us to do things that don't make sense to us, we must be willing to accept the fact that God's thoughts are higher than ours (Isaiah 55:9) and deeper than ours (Psalms 92:5).

Our emotions tell us what we "feel like" doing. Most of us are familiar with how unreliable our emotions can be as a barometer for decision-making. What we feel like doing is not necessarily the right thing for us to do. The obverse is true, as well.

Finally, we should note that the surrender of will, intellect and emotion, through worship, necessarily includes surrender of the "body" because, ultimately, the body does what we "will" it to do. When we surrender in worship, our bodies do as God instructs, for through worship we put God in the driver's seat.

3. Worship is a response to the "God-hood" of God.

In worship, we acknowledge The Divine just because God is "The Great 'I Am.'" "Worship" is a complex word composed of the root-word "worth" and the suffix "-ship." *Worth* means *value*. The suffix *-ship* means *the state of*. In "worship" we acknowledge "the state of God's value." Through worship, we ascribe worth to God. As we worship, we definitively answer this most personal of questions: How much is God worth to you?

As John reminds us in relating the story of the Man Blind from Birth, when we understand Who God is, we are compelled to worship. *See* John 9:38. Remember the wisemen who came to see the Christ-child? When they found Jesus, they fell down and worshiped Him. *See* Matthew 2:11.

4. Worship necessarily involves sacrifice.

The first time that the word "worship" appears in the King James, New International, Revised Standard and New American Standard translations of the Bible is in Genesis 22:5, when Abraham is going to the mountain to sacrifice Isaac. In that verse, Abraham tells his servant to wait, while He and Isaac go to the mountain to "worship." Thus, the concept of "worship" has been inexorably intertwined with the concept of "sacrifice", *ab initio.* There never has been (and there never can be) legitimate worship without sacrifice.

The Relationship Between Worship & Sacrifice

I think it is important that we take this detour through "sacrifice" because this concept is crucial to developing a fuller understanding of praise and worship. Simply defined, <u>sacrifice</u> means *to surrender that which is valuable to God.* There are several principles inherent in the concept of sacrifice that should be addressed in the context of praise and worship:

1. There is no sacrifice, unless that which is offered is given up. Under the Mosaic Law, burnt offerings were burned completely; nothing was left. *See* Leviticus 1

2. Only that which is valuable to the offeror is an acceptable sacrifice from God's perspective.

The first sacrifice mentioned in the Bible is found in Genesis 4, in the story of Cain and Abel. Cain and Abel both presented sacrifices to God. God respected Abel and his offering; however, God did not respect Cain or his offering.

What was the difference between the two offerings? The answer lies in the difference between verse 3 and verse 4: Abel offered the *firstlings* of his flock (v.4), whereas Cain offered the (unmodified) fruit of the ground (v.3)– Abel offered his very best; Cain just offered what was at hand. And notice, God's reaction to the offering and the offeror were the same! Genesis 4: 3-5. How tragic to be "dissed" by the God of the Cosmos! How many of us have missed out on the favor of God because we have offered a paltry sacrifice when it comes to praise and/or worship?

God does not respect a sacrifice that is not valuable to the person giving it, and He does not respect the person who offers a cheap sacrifice. Read II Samuel 24. What was David's response to Arunah's generous offer of free oxen and a free altar?

A sacrifice that isn't valuable to the offeror isn't valuable to God. When God gave instructions on sacrifices under the Mosaic law, He made it clear that He would accept no less than the very best. *See, e.g.,* Leviticus 1:3.

3. *"Worship" always involves "sacrifice."*

I mentioned this briefly before, and we will return to this truth in a more in-depth fashion later. The surrender of will, intellect and emotion in worship is, itself, a sacrifice.

Comparing/Contrasting *Praise* and *Worship*

Based on the material that we have already covered, we can begin to see similarities and differences between the concepts of "praise" and "worship." Here is a list:

1. Praise may be direct or indirect; worship is always direct. Worship is intensely personal and self-reflective, only and always involving two parties: the giver (you or me) and the Object of worship (God).

2. Praise can always be sensed by others; worship may not be so readily identifiable. For example, "fasting" is worship because it involves the surrender of "self." However, "fasting" is neither audible nor visible; thus, it is not praise.)

3. Only Man and angelic beings, who have will, intellect and emotion, can worship God. The whole of creation offers praise. The Psalmist tells us that even nature praises God. Psalms 19:1-5.

4. Generally speaking, praise requires less of us than worship. It is easier to clap my hands than to surrender my "self" (will, intellect, and emotions). Perhaps this is why God seeks worshipers: because they are harder to find. *See* John 4:23.

5. A person who is inhibited in praise will likely be inhibited in worship. Those same inhibitions that hinder us from praising freely, may stand in the way of the surrender of will, intellect and emotions that is essential to worship. If, for example, I am so concerned about what others may think that I cannot stand in praise, how will I ever be able to surrender my "self" in worship?

6. Praise may serve as a prelude to worship, but this is not necessarily so. (In a later example, I Kings 17:8-16, we will see that worship may serve as a prelude to praise)   A brief digression is in order . . .

All too often we treat praise as a pre-game show, while we wait for worship. (As a result, we find ourselves at the benediction, wondering why God didn't show up.) However, worship does not always follow praise. In fact, it is possible to worship (through prayer and fasting, for example) without passing through praise. We must be careful not to limit worship to an "afterglow" that follows praise.

Properly understood, "worship" is much more than an appendix to praise. Worship is a worthy enterprise all its own. Sometimes, it is possible and desirable to praise God without getting into the "worship mode." While using the Outer Court (singing)-Inner Court (praise)- Holy of Holies (worship) paradigm may be helpful in exploring praise and worship in some instances, it can lead to the fictitious belief that [a] worship is superior to praise and/or [b] worship must follow praise.

7. Neither praise nor worship is more important than the other in the life of the Christian.

Tho Word demands that we offer God praise. *See* Psalms 150. God doesn't need our praise. If we are obedient, we will praise God.

God wants us to worship. *See* John 4:23. In fact God is "seeking" worshipers. The Greek word ("zeteo", pronounced "dzay-TEH-o") that is translated "seek" in John 4:23 is the same as that used in the Parable of the the Lost Sheep (Matthew 18:12) and the Parable of the Lost Coin (Luke 15:8). God is on the look-out for worshipers!

8. Praise and worship are both volitional acts. They are voluntary. God does not force them on us; we can decide to praise and/or worship Him or not to do so.

In Isaiah 61:3, the prophet refers to "praise" as a garment. This tells us that "praise" can be put on and it can be taken off, just like any other garment. We can choose to wear "praise." Even when we don't feel like wearing "praise" we can go to our spiritual wardrobe and pull it out.

I have found this to be a true: when I feel least like praising God is really the time that I ought to praise God the most. The prophet Isaiah reminds us that "praise" is a divine remedy for the spirit of heaviness (i.e., depression). In the midst of our lowest, valley-experience, we should consciously put on "praise." The Enemy knows that the spirit of depression can't stand up to praise. Why? Because God is enthroned in our praise. Psalms 22:3. When we praise God, God comes and sits down in the midst of the praise. When God shows up, everything that is not like God must leave!

How do you put on the garment of praise in the midst of your depression? David shows us how in Psalms 103. Read it! Remember Who God is. Magnify Him. Your problems will seem insignificant.

Worship is volitional, too. Why? Because we must consciously surrender our "self." Worship does not happen accidentally. It is a purposeful act, whereby we acknowledge God's "worthy-ship." You can't surrender your will, your intellect, or your emotions inadvertently.

9. We must be careful not to make two mistakes that frequently occur in the praise & worship arena: [1] artificially creating a "praise box" and a "worship box," then trying to force things into one box or the other and [2] being so concerned about getting to the worship "feeling" that we do not worship God. I call this second phenomenon "worshiping worship" because our concern is not so much with God as it is with how we feel. We want a cheap spiritual "high," rather than God's presence.

10. *Finally, we should note that none of these expressions— "praise," "worship" or "praise & worship"— are FEELINGS; rather, they are ACTS.* Certainly these acts must be rooted in and flow from the right "attitude" (i.e. thankfulness).   See Psalm 100:4). However, the way you feel when you praise and/or worship God is unimportant. "Praise" and "worship" are simple expressions. If you lift your hands to God, you have praised God. If you acknowledge God's worth, you have worshiped God.

It's as simple as that.   "Goosebumps do not praise or worship make." Too often we come to church looking for a "feeling" and leave feeling empty. It's not that God's Presence wasn't in the building, and it's not that God did not want to bless us. Rather, it's that we were not in the posture to receive the blessing that God had for us. God had a Word for us, but we didn't hear it. We were too busy looking for a "feeling." God had a Healing for us, but we couldn't receive it. We were too busy looking for a "feeling." Had we stopped "feeling" and started "acting we would have been postured to receive God's blessing. But we were too busy "feeling."

So, why talk about "praise" and "worship" as separate entities? Because, even though the nuances of difference between the two are shades of gray, a clearer understanding of each of the expressions helps one better understand the other.

It is interesting to note that there are some people (and some churches) that have a wonderfully full understanding of "praise," but a very skewed concept of "worship." They'll "dance, dance, dance, dance, dance, dance, dance, all night", but they don't understand (or perhaps don't want to be inconvenienced by) the surrender of self that it takes to "worship." (You know, shout all service long and put $1 in the offering plate.) "Praisers" (and "praising churches"), who don't grasp the concept of worship are like those people who are in love, but can't find it in themselves to make the surrender (i.e., commitment) necessary for marriage. How much more full would the expression of praise (i.e., the lifting of hands, the dance) be if it were directed by God because the lifter/dancer/etc. was lifting/dancing/etc. (not because it was what s/he wanted to do, but) because s/he had surrendered his/her "self" in worship?

On the other side of the coin, there are some people (and some churches) that are great worshipers, but poor praisers. We usually call those people "dry" and refer to the churches that they usually attend "dead" because we don't usually see or hear any praise. Yet, in some instances, those people (and their churches) know how to worship. They regularly surrender their will, intellect and emotion — often through giving liberally. How much more meaningful would their worship be, if it was fueled by the passion of praise?

Perhaps it may be helpful to use "love & marriage" as an analogy to help us better understand the relationship between "praise" and "worship." In both couplets, it is possible to do one without doing the other, but in concert, the whole is greater than the sum of the parts. Love is given fuller expression in marriage, and marriage is made more meaningful because of the passion of love. Similarly, praise is given fuller expression in worship, and worship is made more meaningful because of the passion of praise.

Thus, the phrase "praise & worship" is not completely redundant. The differences between "praise" and "worship" are slight and for the most part hypothetical and academic. It is important to remember that neither is superior to the other and both are ordained of God. From this point, I will try to be consistent in using the phrase "praise & worship," knowing that it is the sum of these "parts" that makes the whole of the "praise & worship" experience we are studying.

II. *Corporate* Praise & Worship

Thus far in our study, our primary focus has been on individual praise & worship, and, quite truthfully, individual praise & worship is important to effective corporate praise & worship. In fact, I believe it is safe to say that, particularly for praise & worship leaders (including "praise team members"), individual praise & worship is essential to effective corporate praise & worship: How can you lead others to a place you have never been? We will return to a more detailed study of individual praise & worship, but for a moment, let's turn to corporate praise & worship. . .

The "Cloud Experience": Paradigm & Pitfall

When looking for models of corporate praise & worship, we often focus on the Chronicler's account of the dedication of Solomon's Temple. *See* II Chronicles 5:12-14. While that passage is a powerful account of what can happen when the people of God come together "as one" in praise & worship, that account is often a fountain of frustration for the New Testament Church because we think that unless we have the "Cloud Experience" every Sunday, we have not worshiped successfully.

A proper, contextual understanding of II Chronicles 5 can help [a] ease our anxiety over trying to re-create the "Cloud Experience" and [b] foster the "atmospheric conditions" conducive to the formation of The Cloud. In worship, God is in the driver's seat, and, no matter what happens, we flow right along with The Divine, instead of trying to direct the course of worship.

Read II Chronicles 5: 1-14. In order to better understand the passage, we must view the Dedication of the Temple in context. Solomon had finished building the Temple, and the Ark was being brought in and set in place. Prior to this time, God's Presence resided in the Tent of Meeting. When God Manifested The Divine Presence there, God did so as a Cloud (or as a Pillar of Fire at night). *See* Exodus 40:34; Numbers 9:15; Deuteronomy 31:15. A review of the previously cited scriptures makes it clear that The Manifestation was not an everyday occurrence. When God did show up as The Cloud, It may have lasted for days, or months at a time or even for a year. Numbers 9:21. But it is clear that The Cloud was not permanent. *See* Numbers 9. Moreover, God's Presence was always in the Tent (because the Ark of the Covenant was there); however, The Cloud was an extraordinary Manifestation visible to all (i.e., not just the high priest on the Day of Atonement), for so long as The Cloud remained.

When we consider the number of times that The Cloud was present in the Tent and the Temple (vis-a-vis the number of worship services held in the Tent and Temple), it becomes clear that it is unrealistic to expect the "Cloud Experience" every time the church doors swing open. Parenthetically, it is interesting to note what Moses recorded in Numbers 9:17-22. We should be mindful that when we do have that Cloud Experience, God may be telling the church "Hold it. I need to give you some instructions for the journey." I digress.

The Cloud Experience was and is relatively rare. To expect it every Sunday is unrealistic and, I submit, is a trick of the Enemy designed to divert our focus from the essence of worship— surrender of self. The Enemy would have us searching for a cloud, rather than surrendering our will, intellect and emotions in reverence to God.

One more point to put The Cloud Experience in context. . .As it is related in II Chronicles 5, The Cloud was a special Sabbath dispensation. God's presence in The Cloud on the day that the Temple was dedicated was an assurance to Israel that God would dwell in the Temple just as God had dwelt in the Tent. *Compare* Exodus 40:34; Number 9:15; II Chronicles 5:13-14. Sometimes when the Lord shows up in an unusual way during a worship service, God is reminding us that The Divine Presence is with us at that time just as in times past.

All of this is not to say we should not expect the Cloud Experience and should not savor the Experience, when it occurs, but whether God manifests as The Cloud in our service or not, God demands praise and seeks worship. We are to offer them.

Before we leave our study of II Chronicles 5, take note of the "when" factor in the passage: God's Presence filled the Temple *when* the singers and musicians (the musical Levites) lifted up praises unto God by singing and playing "as one." The importance of "praise" cannot be understated. If God decides to show up in an unusual way, God will do so in the midst of praise. *See* Psalm 22:3. *Compare* II Chronicles 20. LET THERE BE PRAISE!!!

Just praise God, and let God take care of filling the temple, if that is The Divine Will. Often, instead of praising/worshiping God, we praise/worship a "feeling"— the feeling we had three Sunday's ago when "the Spirit was high." Don't worship worship. Worship God! The truth of the matter is that God manifests The Divine Presence in accordance with The Divine Will..

It is worth repeating: Praise & Worship is not a FEELING; it is an ACT. As Nike says, "Just do it." Do your part; let God take care of The Manifestation.

While we are on the subject of God's Presence in the Temple, let us take a moment for internal reflection. Why? Because the Presence of God, in the Person of the Holy Spirit, now resides within each Believer. The Bible makes it clear that the (individual) Believer is the Temple of the Holy Spirit. *See* I Corinthians 6:19.

Let's back up, before we move forward . . . what happened when the Temple was filled with The Cloud in II Chronicles 5? Right, the priests could not continue to minister. Have you ever been so "full" that you couldn't finish that song you were singing? You just had to stop playing the "shouting music" and dance yourself? That is what happens when His Cloud fills your temple!!!

Read I Peter 2:9. Read it again. Not only are you a temple, you are a priest!!! God can fill your temple at any time and while you are in any place. You don't have to wait until Sunday morning service. You can have a Cloud Experience in the grocery store. When you choose to think of the goodness of God: how the Lord has blessed you, made a way for you, kept you . . . When you surrender your "self" to God, you become a priest worshiping in your own temple.

On Sunday morning, you are temple with a priest coming to a temple with a priest!!! Even when you are in the midst of a worship service with other saints, whether The Cloud is manifested in the service or not, The Cloud can fill your temple. You don't have to wait for the church to get "pumped up." You don't need permission from Bro. Hammond or Sis. Leslie to offer up praise & worship in your temple!

It is worth reemphasizing, however, that whether you have a Cloud Experience in your own temple is God's sovereign decision. God may not move you that way every time. Don't get hooked on the "feeling," get hooked on the "act." God is not seeking the "feeler," He is seeking the "act-er." *See* John 4:23.

Singing Soldiers: The Battle Is Not Yours

Another favorite reference for corporate praise & worship is found in II Chronicles 20, where King Jehosaphat sends the singers out to the battlefield, ahead of the soldiers. Here's the Reader's Digest version of the passage: The kingdom of Judah — "Judah" means "praise"— was facing three enemies. Jehosaphat knew that Judah was outnumbered and would be decimated, unless God intervened. Jehosaphat called for fasting, prayer and praise. As the people praised God, one of the singers (Jahaziel) was moved by the Spirit of God to prophecy that God would fight the battle on behalf of Judah and that all Judah had to do was to "stand still and see the salvation of the Lord. " Trusting this prophetic word, Jehosaphat sent the praise team toward the battlefield in front of the army. As the praise team began to praise & worship, the Lord caused the enemies to destroy each other. Judah won the battle through praise & worship, without drawing a weapon. God "dropped the bomb" on the enemy, while Judah was doing what it had been called to do— praise and worship God.

Judah's praise is obvious from the text: they sang and shouted unto the Lord. But what was their worship? Remember our working definition of "worship"?

Imagine you are part of Judah's praise team, ordered by King Jehosaphat to head toward the battlefield, in front of the army. Think of the surrender of self (will, intellect and emotions) that it took to follow those orders. No sane person wants to be on the front lines of a battle; every intelligent person is aware of the danger of being on the front line; no sensible person "feels" like being on the front line. Yet that is exactly what these people did, and they did so without weapons and without armor.

The Word makes it clear that praise & worship is a weapon in the arsenal of the people of God. When the people praised God in II Chronicles 20, God moved on their behalf against the enemies. This brings us to the popular question: "Why do we need praise leaders and teams in our churches?" ANSWER: The same reason that Jehosaphat appointed them in II Chronicles 20: corporate praise & worship is a weapon to be used in fighting our enemies. The battle must be lead by skilled warriors.

The "praise team" leads the people in praise & worship, that's all. In some churches the deacons fulfill this role, in others there is a song leader. It's not so much what you call the people who lead praise and worship. It's just important that there be an anointed, sanctified leader. When David set up the music ministry, he set certain Levites aside for this specific purpose. All the Levites were to lead the praise, but the musical Levites were specifically called to lead it through singing and playing musical instruments. See II Chronicles 8:14 and I Chronicles 15:16.

Returning to the FEELING v. ACTING motif, notice that the Chronicler does not talk about how the praise team "felt" as they went out to face the vast army without conventional weapons or armor, but he does tell us how they "acted."

Praising Prisoners: Morning at Midnight

What does the New Testament say about praise & worship? Glad you asked. Let's look at Acts 16. Paul and Silas "prayed and sang praises unto God" in jail. They had been placed in jail by the enemies of the church. In the middle of the jailhouse, they started praise & worship. Look what happened. Not only did their praise and worship free them, it freed those around them! Moreover, their praise and worship —remember our definition of "witness" — inspired a former enemy to accept Christ. He even bandaged the wounds that he had inflicted upon them, took them home and fed them. How's that for praise & worship results?!!!

Paul and Silas didn't call for a praise team. They were the praise team. Does the enemy have you in chains? Do you want to break them? Do you want to be delivered from your enemies? Learn to praise Him at our midnight!

The Rev. Dr. Carolyn Showell preaches a life-changing sermon wherein she unveils the Jewish tradition of crying to God during the night watches. In Biblical times, the night was divided into three (3) watches. In the sermon, Dr. Showell explains that Psalms 30:5 ("joy comes in the morning") is a reflection of the fact that in Jewish custom, the people lamented their situations during the first watch, read the Word of God during the second watch and rejoiced over the promises found in the Word of God during the third watch. She goes on to relate that the people became so enraptured in their joyous praise (which began during the third watch) that they were still praising God when the sun rose. Thus joy— their praise— came with the morning!!! Practical application: "morning" begins when, standing on the promises of God, we offer praise. No matter what time of day, no matter what the situation, morning is just a praise away. Paul and Silas knew this. We should remember it, too.

Again, it is worth noting that the Bible doesn't talk how Paul and Silas felt while engaged in praise & worship. (You can imagine how they felt: beaten, thrown in jail . . . But that is not the point. They offered sacrificial praise & worship and God responded. Again, "praise & worship" is NOT a FEELING; it is an ACT.

More Than A Song: Praying for Peter

More New Testament praise & worship . . . read Acts 12. Peter was thrown in jail. The church called a prayer lock-in. The Bible doesn't mention anything about a song being sung, but It does talk about worship. This time worship took the form of prayer. (Study check: Did you catch the worship through fasting in II Chronicles 20?) The prayer in Acts 12 was an "unceasing" prayer. Talk about a grateful surrender of the will, intellect and emotions . . . unceasing prayer on the behalf of a jailed brother.

Now this may be disappointing to those of you who believe that the success or failure of the worship experience is inextricably tied to your vocal ability or your talent on an instrument: the harsh truth of the matter is that the use of your talent is not a necessary prerequisite for worship. More important is the spirit in which the offering is made. Most of us have seen a "rag-tag" looking group of singers with mediocre ability "wreck" a church by offering honest, sincere praise to God. I'll say it again: "Praise & worship" is NOT an enterprise based on how we FEEL; praise and/or worship is/are, purely and simply, ACTs.

In Acts 12, the church was engaged in worship. And they weren't getting together in a church building either. The church— the Body of Believers— was meeting at Mary's house. The individual Believers surrendered their (individual) "self" to God— will, intellect and emotions— and allowed The Divine Presence to fill their individual temples, so that Mary's house was full of filled Temples. As they worshiped, God sent an angel to free Peter. Let's stay with this thought for a moment. Do you know someone who is saved yet bound by the enemy? What kind of miracles would God do on the behalf of bound Christians, if we brought filled Temples to the house of worship?

We are talking about praise & worship. Not just about singing or playing an instrument, we are talking about the effect of individuals surrendering "self" to God in worship. In Acts 12, it was worship in prayer, but it was worship, nonetheless.

III. *Individual* Praise & Worship

By now, it should be clear that corporate praise & worship is simply the collective praise & worship of individuals. (Think of it this way: 100 different instruments tuned to the same note on one piano are all in tune with one another. Corporate worship is properly executed when we are tuned, individually, to praise & worship which is in tune with The Divine.) While we tend to focus on corporate praise & worship because [a] that's what happens in church and [b] most of us are not committed to a lifestyle of praise & worship, the importance of individual praise & worship cannot be overemphasized, for there can be no corporate praise & worship, unless there is individual praise & worship

"So," you ask, "why do I (personally) need to engage in praise & worship?" We have already addressed the fact that God commands us to praise Him and that He seeks worshipers. That, in and of itself, should be enough. II Chronicles 20 gives us another reason.

As did the children of Israel in II Chronicles 20, we have spiritual enemies. One of the weapons to be used in fighting against our enemies is praise & worship. There are some battles in our lives that God wants to fight on our behalf. If we would learn to engage in praise & worship and to let God take care of those II Chronicles 20-type battles that we face, we could avoid many unnecessary battle scars.

Sometimes God wants to move on our behalf, but we are too busy rushing to engage the enemy in our own strength. At those times, we should "stand still" and give God space to "set an ambush" on our enemies. We should praise God on the way to the battlefield. Stop trying to fight your enemies in your own power. The prophecy of Jahaziel resounds across time and throughout eternity: "The battle is not yours; it's the Lord's."

Let's look at a few *individual* praise & worship archetypes...

Worship By A Sinner: Luke 7:36-50

> 36 And one of the Pharisees desired him that he would eat
> with him. And he went into the Pharisee's house, and sat
> down to meat.
> 37 And, behold, a woman in the city, which was a sinner,
> when she knew that Jesus sat at meat in the Pharisee's house,
> brought an alabaster box of ointment,
> 38 And stood at his feet behind him weeping, and began to
> wash his feet with tears, and did wipe them with the hairs
> of her head, and kissed his feet, and anointed them with
> the ointment.
> * * *
> 48 And he said unto her, Thy sins are forgiven.

Wow! Now that's worship ~t it's finest and led by a sinner, no less.
Talk about the surrender of will, intellect and emotion.

[a] will: She could have been out on the street earning her liv-
ing, but she "willed" herself to be in Jesus presence.

[b] intellect: She broke open a box of precious ointment and
anointed Jesus feet. The ointment was probably her life-sav-
ings and was worth somewhere in the neighborhood of $20,000.
Some things just don't make sense to the carnal mind.

[c] emotions: In earnest sorrow for her sins and in recognition
of Jesus' holiness, she cried so much so that she "washed" his
feet with her tears.

Before we discuss some of the finer points of this worship paradigm, I would like to reemphasize one point: in its purest form,
worship is an all-or-nothing proposition. The sacrifice that is part
and parcel of worship is "no holds barred." As noted above, when
the principal character in the Luke 7 story opened the alabaster box,
she poured it all out!!! Remember that under the Levitical law the
entire sacrifice had to be offered up. None of the offering could be
left. *See* Leviticus 1.

It is worth noting (again) that the very first sacrifice that carried the connotation of worship— Abraham sacrificing Isaac in Genesis 22:5— required that the object offered in worship be sacrificed *in toto*. Abraham had to be willing to give up everything. Abraham's sacrifice would be more than Isaac. Abraham had to be willing to give up the only tangible evidence of God's promise to him and to his wife. And let's not overlook Isaac' sacrifice. Isaac's worship was found in his decision to <u>willingly</u> lay down his life. (Abraham could not have forced Isaac to submit to being tied up, placed on an altar and killed. Abraham was a senior citizen when Isaac was conceived.)

The sacrifices of Abraham and Isaac give a clear answer to the worship's question, "How much do you value God?" Both Abraham and Isaac answer: "I value God more than life, itself." What a tremendous sacrifice was required: will, intellect and emotions screamed, NO. But a worshiper– an Abraham, an Isaac, an un-named woman with an alabaster box– can only respond with a YES. When we come to the realization that God is worthy– truly worthy– the complete surrender of that which we hold most dear is of no consequence. God is worthy of TOTAL praise, TOTAL worship.

The practical challenge for us is this: are we willing to sacrifice our "Isaac" on the altar in worship; are we willing to lay down our lives; are we willing to break our alabaster box? Worship God in Spirit and in Truth. There is the Divine Promise of a ram in the bush and the ointment you pour out for God is insignificant, when compared with the Anointing that God will pour in you. Lose yourself in worship: true worship, full worship, total worship.

Let us return to the narrative of the unnamed worshiper in Luke 7. I'd like to highlight two easily overlooked aspects of her radical worship:

1. *Her worship inadvertently attracted the attention of others, most of whom misunderstood it.*

It seems clear that she did not worship Jesus for the purpose of attracting (human) attention to herself. Sure, she wanted Jesus' attention, and, because of her worship, that is exactly what she got. Whether the Pharisee were there or not, I believe her action— her surrender of "self"— would have been the same. When the Pharisee saw her crying, wiping Jesus feet with her hair, then kissing and anointing his feet, they couldn't help but notice what she was doing, and it was this fact that annoyed them. ("Now when the Pharisee which had bidden him saw it, he spake within himself, saying, This man, if he were a prophet, would have known who and what manner of woman this is that toucheth him: for she is a sinner." Luke 7:39.)

Worship will attract the attention of others, many of whom will wonder why you are doing what you are doing and many of whom will misunderstand your intention. More than anything, fear of what other's may think binds us in praise & worship. But the reality is that the object of our worship, The Triune God, is present and understands! That is more than enough!

2. *She did not let the fact that she was a sinner keep her from approaching God.*

The importance of this observation cannot be understated. Why? Because it assures us that we can approach God in worship, even though there is sin in our lives. Some people believe that they can only worship God when they are sin-free. NOT SO!! If being sin-free were a prerequisite, none of us could ever worship. Sin is an inextricable part of the human life-experience. No matter how mature we are in Christ, sin is ever present. As God told Cain, before Cain killed Abel, "sin lieth at the door" for every one of us.

The Apostle John puts it this way:

> 8 If we say that we have no sin, we deceive ourselves, and the truth is not in us.
> 9 If we confess our sins, he is faithful and just to forgive us our sins, and to cleanse us from all unrighteousness.
> 10 If we say that we have not sinned, we make him a liar, and his word is not in us.

I John 1:10, echoing Romans 3:23, makes it clear that we have all sinned (past tense). But I John 1:8 makes it clear that each of us has sin (present tense) in our lives. There is no sense in deceiving ourselves: you and I have sin. Face it! You are not as sanctified as you think you are!

The good news is that God is faithful and just to forgive us our sins, and, moreover, promises to cleanse us from all unrighteousness. I John 1:9. Jesus told Peter to forgive an individual who sinned against him (Peter) as often as the individual asked for it. See Matthew 18:22. If God expects that of us, can we not expect that of Him?

This is not to say that "worship" is some type of "quick-fix," substitute for grace. God will not accept hypocritical worship, and the hypocritical worshiper risks losing the favor of God. See Genesis 4 and I Samuel 15:24-31. The only acceptable worship takes place in "spirit and truth"; thus, "worship" requires the highest integrity on the part of the worshiper. The point of this discussion is to make it clear that when we fall prey to sin, we ought not compound the problem by separating ourselves from God. In those times— and we all have them— we need to [a] confess our sin and [b] draw near to God through worship. As we confess, God forgives us. As we worship surrendering our all to The Divine, God cleanses us. And the cleansing that God performs addresses more than just the sin issue that brings us to the point of confession. In cleansing us, God softens our hardened hearts, shaping us more and more in the Divine image, cleansing us not just from the sin we were focusing at the confession, but from all the unrighteousness in our lives.

The Bible makes it clear that we are not to misuse the Saving Grace of the Blood as an excuse to continue in sin (see Romans 6:1), but even as we learn to forget those things that are behind us– things that were part of our lives before we were convicted by the Spirit to know that they were sin– and "press toward the mark," God stands ready to accept our worship.

Don't let Satan trick you into believing you are too sinful to worship God. You and I are sinners, but, if you have accepted Jesus as Savior, you and I are saved sinners: free from the spirit of condemnation, by the blood of Jesus. Romans 8:1.

More On Individual Worship

These next two examples of individual worship– "Worship Through Following God" and "Worship Through Giving"– are acts of worship that are often not associated with "praise & worship." It's not that the Church Traditional does not follow God and/or does not give. Rather, generally speaking, we do not associate these acts– wherein we surrender will, intellect and emotion– with the word "worship."

The church tends to limit "worship" to a feeling that follows "good singing" or "good preaching." Since "good singing" and "good preaching" usually happen during church service, we tend toward a skewed vantage about what worship is. As a consequence, we tend to miss out on the blessing of worshiping, as CeCe Winans sings, "Alone In His Presence." To round out the material presented, here, I think it is important to look at these two forms of worship for at least three reasons:

[a] worship is a lifestyle choice, which, when properly understood, is not relegated to the Sunday morning experience;

[b] worship need not be an "addendum" to praise; and

[c] God has promised specific blessings to those who practice these forms of worship.

I will leave it to the reader to reason through [a] and [b]. However, I hope to discuss, with some specificity, the blessings promised by God for those who worship through following and through giving.

It is also my hope that our discussion will go a long way toward keeping those who (over-) emphasize praise as the doorway to worship– where we only worship after we praise– from dismissing as "unspiritual" those people (and churches) that they think of as "dead." Similarly, I hope that the material presented on "praise" will help those who under-emphasize praise to understand why "it takes all of 'that' and more" to praise God. As we discussed earlier, the combination of "praise & worship" is greater than the sum of its parts and God has ordained that we do both.

a. Worship Through Following: Matthew 4:18-22

> 18And Jesus, walking by the sea of Galilee, saw two
> brethren, Simon called Peter, and Andrew his brother,
> casting a net into the sea: for they were fishers.
> 19And he saith unto them, Follow me, and I will make
> you fishers of men.
> 20And they straightway left their nets, and followed him.
> 21And going on from thence, he saw other two brethren,
> James the son of Zebedee, and John his brother, in a ship
> with Zebedee their father, mending their nets; and he
> called them.
> 22And they immediately left the ship and their father,
> and followed him.

Here we see another example of worship– the surrender of will, intellect and emotion in response to the revelation by God of God's Self and The Divine Will. These two sets of brothers left their professions and strained family ties to follow Jesus. This is the quintessential paradigm of "worship through following."

To worship through following, means to travel the path that God has called us to walk. In Psalms 37, the Psalmist writes,

> 3Trust in the LORD, and do good; [so] shalt thou dwell
> in the land, and verily thou shalt be fed.
> 4 Delight thyself also in the LORD; and he shall give
> thee the desires of thine heart.
> 5Commit thy way unto Him and he shall bring [it] to
> pass.

Notice the progressive nature of the promises that God gives to us:

[a] Trust God; God promises to meet our needs.
[b] Delight in God (i.e., praise God; *see* Isaiah 58:13-14); God promises to give us our hearts' desire (i.e., our dreams).
[c] Follow God; God promises to move sovereignly on our behalf.

Look again at verse 5. According to Strong's Concordance, the Hebrew word translated "way" [derek; DEH-rek] means "road; way; path; course of life." The Hebrew word translated "bring [it] to pass" [asah; aw-SAW] is a verb and means "to do; to execute." Verse 5 says clearly that God has promised to move sovereignly on the behalf of those who worship by following the Divinely ordained path for their lives. God will "bring to pass."

What will God bring to pass? "It!"

What is the "it"? The "it" is whatever God has planned for us: more than meeting our needs, more (even) than granting our dreams. God is able "to do exceeding abundantly above all that we ask or think." Ephesians 3:20.

Again we return to the principle that worship is personal and simple!!! It's NOT a FEELING; it is an ACT—it's the surrendering of "self."

b. Worship Through Giving: I Kings 17: 8-16

8 And the word of the LORD came unto him, saying,
9 Arise, get thee to Zarephath, which belongeth to Zidon, and dwell there: behold, I have commanded a widow woman there to sustain thee.
10 So he arose and went to Zarephath. And when he came to the gate of the city, behold, the widow woman was there gathering of sticks: and he called to her, and said, Fetch me, I pray thee, a little water in a vessel, that I may drink.
11 And as she was going to fetch it, he called to her, and

said, Bring me, I pray thee, a morsel of bread in thine hand.
12 And she said, As the LORD thy God liveth, I have not a
cake, but an handful of meal in a barrel, and a little oil in a
cruse: and, behold, I am gathering two sticks, that I may go
in and dress it for me and my son, that we may eat it, and
die.
13 And Elijah said unto her, Fear not; go and do as thou
hast said: but make me thereof a little cake first, and bring it
unto me, and after make for thee and for thy son.
14 For thus saith the LORD God of Israel, The barrel of meal
shall not waste, neither shall the cruse of oil fail, until the
day that the LORD sendeth rain upon the earth.
15 And she went and did according to the saying of Elijah:
and she, and he, and her house, did eat many days.
16 And the barrel of meal wasted not, neither did the cruse
of oil fail, according to the word of the LORD, which he
spake by Elijah.

Worship? Definitely! It has all the elements of worship. The Lord
commanded a widow, who had a young son and enough food left for
one meal, to provide food and water to a prophet in the middle of
drought and famine, and she did it! Her will, intellect and emotions
screamed "NO!" But she surrendered to God.

And look at God! She worshiped and God took what she gave
and He gave it back to her in abundance. Talk about "good measure,
pressed down, shaken together and running over!" (Luke 6:38) In the
middle of a famine, she had flour and oil.

I can imagine that a "praise" followed this act of "worship." It
bears repeating: "Praise & worship" is NOT a FEELING; it's an ACT.
The widow gave and God responded; He will do the same for us.

IV. Leading Corporate Praise & Worship

Now we turn to the praise leader and/or praise team: those who lead the congregation in praise & worship. While praise & worship is for everyone, leading it is not. Only praisers and worshipers need apply!

This is not a ministry for those who have not committed themselves to a lifestyle of "praise & worship" that goes beyond the Sunday morning "party." And it is not for those who are not willing to prepare themselves in private for the battle that they lead in the public worship service. Let's examine a few of the things that every praise & worship leader must know, if he or she is to be effective.

<u>"Ministry"</u>

Simply defined, a ministry is anything that meets a need in the body of Christ. When there is corporate worship, the Body definitely needs to be led in praise & worship. The Old Testament tells us that it was the general duty of the Levites to lead the praise and to assist the priests. II Chronicles 8:14. All of the Old Testament musicians and singers were Levites, and there were assigned to sing the Word of God, while accompanied by musical instruments. I Chronicles 15:16; I Chronicles 25. This was their ministry and they took it seriously. All of them were trained and skilled in music for the Lord. I Chronicles 25:8

<u>The "Call" to Ministry</u>

What does it mean to be called? For the musical Levites of the Old Testament, it meant being born into the right family and being born male. What does it mean now, under the New Covenant? Read Acts 13. (Also, see Galations 3:28 with respect to the "gender issue."

To be "called" is to be set apart by God for ministry. Acts 13 provides the quintessential example of being called to ministry. Note first that God, in the Person of the Holy Spirit, sends out the call to ministry. A close reading of Acts 13 , makes it clear that being "saved" and even being "saved and spiritual" is not the same as being "called" to a specific ministry. Look at what happened to John Mark.

John Mark went with Paul and Barnabas on their missionary journey. But by verse 13, John Mark leaves them and apparently does so without notice (*see* Acts 15:38). Why? John Mark had not been called to serve in that particular ministry venture.

Now, this is the same John Mark who wrote the Gospel of Mark. He was saved. He was Spirit-filled. But John Mark was not called to the missionary journey in Acts 13, and when things got rough– things will get rough in ministry– he couldn't persevere. The Holy Spirit calls specific persons to do a specific work. It wasn't that John Mark wasn't a good person; he simply wasn't called. He had no anointing to do that ministry.

We are anointed by God so that we are empowered to do the ministry that God has called us to. Jesus, Himself, was anointed to do ministry. Acts 10:38. He was called and anointed to do a specific work. Luke 4:18. In fact "Christ," means "Anointed One." If Christ had to be anointed to succeed in ministry, it stands to reason that we need to be anointed to minister through the medium of praise & worship, if we are to be successful?

I suspect that John Mark wanted to minister with Paul and Barnabas (otherwise, why would he have gone?), but God had not anointed John Mark for that ministry at that time. Sure, John Mark was on fire for the Lord. But being excited about Jesus is not enough. If we are to be effective praise & worship leaders, leading praise & worship must be our calling. You've got to know beyond a doubt that you are answering God's call on your life, when you stand before the people of God and lead them in corporate praise & worship. Otherwise, 13 verses later, you'll find yourself in John Mark's situation.

Being A Leader

Let's begin this phase of our study by stating two important truths: (1) a praise team is more than a bunch of singers and (2) a singer is not necessarily a praise & worship leader. Praise & worship is not tight, slamming harmonies nor is it exciting the folks with your vocal riffs and runs. Praise & worship is "getting into God's nostrils" by offering a sacrifice that God accepts as sweet savor. *See, e.g.,* Leviticus 1:9. *Compare* Amos 5:23. To lead praise and worship effectively, one must be willing to offer "naked praise" to God in front of the people of God.

In addition, to being called, a praise & worship leader must be willing to lead. This means that as individuals, we must be committed to a lifestyle of praise & worship. It is axiomatic, "if you haven't been there, you can't lead someone else there." You may be in front when the group arrives at the destination, but that doesn't mean that you have led. (And it goes, without saying, that you cannot lead people from behind.)

Praise and worship, for the praise & worship leader, must always be a matter of leading by example: "Oh magnify the Lord with me. Let us exalt God's Name together!" Some people misinterpret this to mean that the praise & worship leader must be a spiritual cheerleader: trying to get the people "pumped up and primed" for praise and worship. That is a shallow misinterpretation of the role of the praise & worship leader. It's not so much trying to excite the people into praise & worship; rather, it's leading them by example. As leaders, we ought to be first to lift our hands. We ought to be the first to shout unto the Lord for joy. We ought to be the first to praise Him in the dance. We should do these things, not because the people will get excited, but because we know "God is good and God's mercy endureth forever." *See* Psalms 136.

If the praise team only "gets happy" when the congregation "gets happy," something is wrong. We have not led. We just happened to arrive at the same destination at the same time.

The Prophetic Nature of Music Ministry

Much of our leading as praise & worship leaders will take the form of music. It's not that songs should be the singular focal point of our praise and worship, but musical praise is, more often than not, the gateway through which we enter worship, particularly corporate worship. With that in mind, it is important that we know something about the purpose and nature of music ministry. We have discussed that praise (whether in the form of music or otherwise) is two-dimensional in scope and effect: both [a] directed toward God and [b] sensed by man. We have covered the God-directed aspects of praise in other parts of this material. Let us now turn to the second dimension of praise. In particular, let's look at the principal indirect attribute of musical praise: prophecy. (Also, known as "eavesdropping" because the congregation eavesdrops on the leaders conversation with The Divine. See Psalm 149:1.)

What is "prophecy"? According to I Corinthians 14:3, prophecy is simple. It is speaking the word of God for the purpose of edifying, exhorting and comforting others. Strong's Concordance give the following definitions of the key words found in I Corinthians 14:3: [a] "to edify" means "to build up, as in promoting growth" [b] "to exhort" means "to encourage through oratory discourse"; and [c] "to comfort" means "to console." Prophecy is not just foretelling; in principal part, it is forthtelling: speaking God's word by Divine Inspiration.

It is clear that since its initiation in I Chronicles 25, the music ministry has been a prophetic ministry. Each of the three original ministers of music— Asaph, Heman and Ethan (Jeduthun)— and their sons were set apart (i.e., "called") to prophesy accompanied by musical instruments. Thus, it is clear that, when there is both vocal and instrumental music, the instrumental music plays a secondary role. The voices are primary for the prophecy must be heard above the music. As at the dedication of the Temple, the singers and musicians should be making "one sound to be heard in praising and thanking the Lord." II Chronicles 5:13.

Because the prophecy is primary, we must be certain that the songs that we sing are prophetic in nature. The fact that we like a song, or that it's popular, or that it has a good beat, or "phat" chords, does not mean that it is prophetic. Some of the things that we sing would be better left unsung.

A principal issue to be addressed is this: what is the prophetic content of the music that we sing during praise & worship. As we prepare for corporate praise & worship, the leader must take seriously the prophetic nature of the music ministry: what does God want to say to through the music? Are we allowing God to speak through us? Are we just choosing songs that what we like? Are we just choosing songs that we haven't sung in a while? Do the songs have a central unifying theme? Are the songs in line with the liturgical calendar? Do they reinforce the Pastor's current series of sermons? There's more to it than first appears. As every good prophet knows, "you've got to seek before you speak." This applies to the praise team, too.

The Role of Instrumental Music in Praise and Worship

The Bible makes it clear that the playing of musical instruments is, itself, praise. See Psalms 150. (The playing of an instrument becomes worship when the musician makes his/her offering, because s/he acknowledges God's worth.) The Bible also makes it clear that praise is a weapon to be used in spiritual warfare. See II Chronicles 20 (Jehosaphat and the singing soldiers, supra)

When a called musician takes his/her place at the instrument, he or she pulls another weapon out of God's arsenal. And what an effective weapon it is. Look at its effect on demon-oppressed Saul. I Samuel 16:23. Look at how it affected Elisha when he was too upset to deliver a Word from God. II Kings 3:15.

Lyrics and vocal riffs did not chase the demon from Saul. The Bible is clear (and the Hebrew bears it out) that David played the harp with his hand and, thus, drove away the demon. David could sing, but he wasn't singing when he soothed Saul's troubled mind.

The same word "nagan" [naw-GAN] that is used to describe David's playing in I Samuel 16:23 is used three times in II Kings 3:15 and is translated as the noun "minstrel" and as the verb "played." It is clear, again, that Elisha's breakthrough followed instrumental music, without vocals.

There are times in praise & worship, when the breakthrough comes through instrumental music. Just music. No voices. Just music. Singers must learn to be sensitive to those times, just as the musicians must be sensitive when accompanying the singers. Singers must learn to yield not only at the "shout," when the dancers are "getting their step in," but even in those calm, quiet moments. Listen! You may hear the sound of the spiritual battle.

And while we're on the subject, when the music lingers beyond the song, that's not always exit music for the praise team. There's a battle going on! Singers, if you are returning to your seats do it with reverence and as unobtrusively as possible. We're not talking about respecting the musician, we're talking about recognizing that in the midst of a battle one false move can mean the difference between victory and defeat. Even if it's not your battle, know that somebody in the congregation may be having a Saul experience. They need to hear the music! The preacher may need the minstrel so he or she can deliver a Word from God.

Finally, every musician must understand that his/her instrument is a battle station. Through their fingers, they fire a powerful spiritual weapon. It is not a talent. It is a weapon. And the more skilled we become at using the weapon, the more effective we become at making war. Look at what David, the warrior-musician says: "Blessed be the LORD my strength which teacheth my hands to war, and my fingers to fight." Psalms 144:1.

V. Concluding Thoughts

"Praise" and "worship" are separate, yet interrelated, concepts. Developing an understanding and an appreciation for them individually and in the form of "praise & worship" is important. Praise & Worship is MORE THAN a FEELING. It is an ACT: an act consecrated by God. God has given us instructions in The Word as to how we are to offer praise and worship. We need only follow the instructions.

There is more to praise & worship than lifting our hand or singing or playing an instrument. Praise & Worship begins with the right attitude: that is, an "attitude of gratitude." Yet it goes beyond (and at times ignores) how we feel. It is truly a lifestyle of acting out the gratefulness that is in our hearts (i.e., "praise") and surrendering our "self" to God (i.e., "worship").

God has called all of us to be praisers and to be worshipers. And it is not God's intent that praise & worship be limited in time and scope to a Sunday morning experience. The Bible says that God is to be praised "from the rising of the sun unto the going down of the same." Psalms 113:3. A common, superficial interpretation of that verse is chronological— praise God from morning until night. But this interpretation leaves a gaping hole in our theology: What about when night has come, shall we not praise God?

Two other interpretations of Psalms 113:3 are more encompassing and more relevant to the body of Christ. First, instead of limiting ourselves to *chronos*, let us look at Psalm 113:3 from God's perspective on time. Read II Peter 3:8. God's operates in "*kairos.*" Thus, our praise should be on His timetable. In other words, God is to be praised from the dawning of time throughout eternity. The heavenly host do it, and we, the saints of God, have a redemption story that they can never have. *See also* Hebrews 13:15. Second, it is also fitting that for our omnipresent God, we look at Psalms

113:3 from a spatial perspective— God is to be praised from the place the sun rises (i.e., the East) the place where it sets (i.e., the West). *See* Psalms 113:3 [NIV] In other words, God is to be praised all the time and everywhere.

God has anointed some of us to lead the corporate praise and worship. God also has called others of us to serve as singing prophets and as musicians, unleashing the power of praise [a] in our own lives, [b] in the lives of God's people and [c] in the lives of those who don't know Jesus as Lord and Savior. Serving God as a praise and worship leader– whether as a singer or as a musician– requires a lifestyle of sacrificial praise and worship. Praise & Worship is more than a song. We are warriors engaged in a battle, and "we wrestle not against flesh and blood." Ephesians 6:12. Warfare requires the use of various weapons and skill in knowing which weapon to use at what time. Praise & Worship may take the form of singing, but it also may take the form of fasting, praying, playing instrumental music, giving a liberal offering, etc. It takes all kinds of spiritual weapons to fight this battle. Praise & Worship is only one weapon, but it is a powerful weapon.

LET THERE BE PRAISE AND WORSHIP!!!

VI. Epilogue: "Triple-Point" –
A Thankful Heart, Praise, and Worship

Psalms 100:4 Enter into His gates with thanksgiving, and into His courts with praise: be thankful
unto Him, and bless His Name.

God has chosen to reveal The Divine Self to us through The Bible. In seeking to understand the Word of God, we must begin with prayer. God is faithful to give a clear understanding of The Word to those who prayerfully seek The Holy Ghost, as Teacher. But Paul admonishes us not merely to pray for understanding of the Word of God, but also to "study to show ourselves approved unto God . . . rightly dividing [or handling] the Word of truth." (II Timothy 2:15).

The Holy Ghost does not teach in a vacuum. Often God teaches us by compelling us to search for understanding. This is what Solomon is speaking of when he says, "It is the glory of God to conceal a thing: but the honor of kings to search out a matter." (Proverbs 25:2). We are made monarchs through the blood of Jesus. (Revelations 1:6). For the next few moments, we will claim our royal birthright, as we search out the matter of "praise & worship" by examining Psalms100:4.

In many instances, God uses what we have learned in other fields of study to help us understand the mystery of His Word. To better understanding the instant text, I would propose that we use two tools from our school days: grammar and literary interpretation.

In order to develop a more complete understanding of what the psalmist is saying to us in Psalms 100:4 and to grasp its relevance to "praise & worship," I want to take you back to elementary school English and on a brief journey into middle school poetry. Indulge me for a moment, as the Holy Ghost leads us in this quest to understand more about this thing we call "praise & worship."

First, grammar . . . If we were editing Psalms100:4 today, we would most likely divide it into three sentences: one sentence for each independent thought –

> [a] Enter into His gates with thanksgiving and into His courts with praise.
> [b] Be thankful unto Him.
> [c] Bless His Name.

Based on these three sentences, we're going to "diagram" this verse the old-fashioned way. We will look, for a moment, at verbs and nouns and objects and prepositions in order to develop a clear understanding of the message of the verse.

[a] **Enter into God's gates with thanksgiving and into God's courts with praise.** The verb in the first sentence is "enter." It is a literal translation of the Hebrew root word *bow* (pronounced BO). In the Hebrew, the verb is used in the imperative mood, and, thus, is a command: a command "to enter." The two conjoined prepositional phrases (beginning with the word "with") – "with thanksgiving" and "with praise" – serve as adverbs, explaining how were are to enter God's gates and courts. "Thanksgiving" and "praise" are the objects of the prepositional phrases. They are nouns, representing "things" as opposed to "actions." The only action in this sentence is the command "enter."

Let's return the full phrase for a closer look: this time through the lens of the poet. To enter God's gates and courts is symbolic of approaching God's Presence. In the Old Testament, a person who approached the house of the Lord – Tabernacle or Temple – had to approach by entering first into the gates and then into the courts. The courts could be divided into two broad categories: the Outer Court and the Inner Court. The Presence of God dwelt in the house of the Lord, above the Ark of Covenant. The Ark was in the Most Holy Place, behind the veil at the far end of the Inner Court. To get there, one had to travel (first) through the gates and (then) through the Outer Court and (ultimately) through the Inner Court. By referencing the gates and the courts, David is painting a "word picture" on the subject of approaching God. David also gives us detailed instruction as to how we are to approach God.

By telling us to "[e]nter into His gates with thanksgiving and into His courts with praise," the psalmist commands the listener (the implied subject) to approach God with certain things in his/her possession – thanksgiving and praise: **things not actions**. In fact the NIV translation of the Bible, notes that "with thanksgiving" may better be translated "with a thank offering." In other words, we are to approach God, carrying thanksgiving and praise. Where do we place the things that we carry? We place them in our hearts, approaching God with hearts filled with thanksgiving and praise – "thankful hearts."

(I will use the phrase "thankful hearts" throughout the remainder of this discussion to refer to hearts filled with thanksgiving and praise.)

[b] **Be thankful (Give thanks) unto God.** The word translated "be thankful" in English, is one word in Hebrew. The Hebrew root word is *yadah* [yaw-DAW]. Ordinarily, *yadah* is a noun; however, the Psalmist has carefully chosen a form of *yadah*, which clearly indicates that the word being used as a verb. As it is used here, however, the stem of the word *yadah* is in a form that is used to make a noun into a verb. In English, it's like taking the noun "thanks" and making it into the verb-phrase "give thanks." In fact most other translations of this passage render the form of the verb *yadah* used here, "give thanks."

Make a mental note. We will return to this point later: there is a difference between "having a thankful heart" and "giving thanks."

[c] **Bless God's Name.** *Barak* [baw-RAK] is the root form of the verb translated "bless." It is used here in a form that indicates intensive and intentional action. To bless something is to speak well of that thing, but what does it mean to "Bless God's Name?"

To answer this question, we need to understand the significance of a person's name in Hebrew culture. In that culture, a person's name is believed to be an encapsulation of his/her unique, salient character trait. To bless someone's name, then, is to speak well of that person's character. It is an acknowledgment of that person's uniqueness. Blessing a person's name, acknowledges that person's worth. Thus, "Blessing the Name of the Lord" is to acknowledge God's worth, which is the essence of worship.

And so . . . you have survived sentence diagraming and even done a little bit of poetry . . . and I hope that we have laid a firm groundwork for discussion of the interrelationship among [a] the thankful heart, [b] praise, and [c] worship.

Often Psalms100:4 is used to illustrate a linear, segmented progression from thanksgiving to praise and (ultimately) to worship: [1] thanksgiving in the gates; [2] followed by praise in the courts; [3] culminating in worship in the Most Holy Place. The hermeneutic problem with this interpretation is that it implies that the verse is not universal in the applicability of its command, particularly the command to worship God. Specifically, the "progression theory" implies that worship occurs only the Most Holy Place. At the time David wrote this psalm, only the high priest could enter the Most Holy Place. If Psalms100:4 is interpreted to mean that one progresses from thanksgiving in the gates to worship in Most Holy Place, then (it necessarily follows that) only one person could really worship in the Old Testament dispensation – the high priest. Thus, David's psalm could only have been understood as a psalm to be sung by the high priest. But this was not the case. All the people sung Psalm 150, It was part of the Jewish hymn book! I submit that viewing these three concepts – [a] the thankful heart, [b] praise, and [c] worship – as segmented steps that are somehow related to the layout of the Temple or Tabernacle cannot be a correct interpretation of scripture. There must be some other hermenuetic principle by which we may interpret the lyric of this Psalm.

Let's get some basic definitions out of the way and associate them directly with our scripture reference:

THANKFUL HEART – Recall that we are using this phrase to summarize the conjoined prepositional phrases – "with thanksgiving" and "with praise" – contained in Psalms100:4: the phrases that tell what we must bring when we approach God. Every acceptable offering to God – praise and worship are offerings, you know – springs forth from a thankful heart. A person who doesn't have a thankful heart will never praise or worship God, because he or she will never see the point. But when a person praises and worships God, he or she becomes thankful all over again and this leads him or her to worship and to praise God, which leads them to be thankful. . . . But I'm getting ahead of myself.

PRAISE – The concept of praise appears twice in this verse. First as a noun (". . . with **praise**") and undercover in the verb-phrase "give thanks" or "be thankful." We have addressed the noun form (along with thanksgiving) under the heading "thankful heart." In the noun-sense, praise is not something that we do; rather, it is something we have. We might equate "having praise" with "having a testimony," whereas "giving a praise" is like "giving a testimony." "Having" and "giving" are two different things. "Having" does not require any action; "giving" necessarily does. "Having" is an excellent place to begin. In fact, as we have already discussed, "having" is a necessary precondition to "giving," when it comes to praise. For without a thankful heart, one cannot praise God.

"Praise" occurs in verb-form in our text wrapped in the concept of "be[ing] thankful" or (more correctly translated to indicate action) "giv[ing] thanks." This grammatical fact is important because, from a Biblical perspective, praise necessarily requires audible and/or visible action on the part of the praiser.

To praise means "to commend; to express approval or admiration; to extol in word or song or deed." Thus, one praises when one commends, expresses approval or admiration, or extols God. Merely carrying the praise on the inside is not enough. Having a thankful heart is a good place to start, but we are commanded to do more than have a thankful heart. We are also commanded to give thanks. At some point, the thankfulness that we have in our hearts must break forth into action, whereby we give praise to God.

Not convinced that praise must be visible and/or audible? Remember Jesus' ride into Jerusalem on that first Palm Sunday? The Bible says in Luke 19:37 "the whole multitude of the disciples began to rejoice and praise God with a loud voice for all the mighty works that they had seen." The Bible further relates that the Pharisees got upset about all the commotion. Jesus told them this: "...if these should hold their peace, the stones would immediately cry out." (v. 40) As the Psalmist says, we are to make the voice of God's praise to be heard. Psalms 66:8.

WORSHIP - Worship is an act by a redeemed man or woman (the creature) toward God (the Creator) whereby his/her will, intellect and emotions gratefully respond in reverence, honor and devotion to the continuing revelation by God of His Person and His Will. In other words, worship is the grateful surrender of self – will, intellect and emotions – to God. We give our desires, thoughts and feelings over to Him. When we worship, we submit our will to His Will; we acknowledge that His thoughts are higher and deeper than our thoughts (Isaiah 55:9 & Psalms 92:5), and recognize that what He wants is what is best for us. Worship is, in point of fact, the sacrifice of "self." This explains why true worshipers are such rare commodities that God is "seeking" them. John 4:23

We see the concept of worship in the command to "Bless His Name." Let me correct a misconception. Merely saying, "You are The Lord. I worship You" or reciting a Name of God is not worship. Worship is more than speech, no matter how rapidly or how loudly one speaks. Worship requires action. Worship is action that acknowledges God's Lordship. It's fine to say "You are the Lord." But the real question is this: Do my life's choices reflect God's Lordship? Saying that God is "Jehovah Jireh" is one thing. Stepping out on faith and giving an offering that logic says I cannot afford to give, but that God has asked me to give anyway, that's worship. Saying that God is "The Lord Mighty in Battle" is one thing. Allowing The Lord to fight my battles, instead of me trying to fight them according to my power or might , that's worship.

Worship is Andrew, Peter, James and John leaving their families and their livelihoods to take up with a carpenter-turned-itinerant-preacher from Nazareth. (Matthew 4) Worship is the Widow of Zarephath making a loaf of bread for the prophet, before preparing a last supperl for herself and her child. (I Kings 17) Worship is Abraham and Isaac going to a mountain, knowing that the Lord would provide a sacrifice. (Genesis 22).

Worship is more than speech; it is the grateful, voluntary surrender of self. The act of self-sacrifice is the act that blesses the Name of the Lord. Worship is any act that says to God, "I know Your Name; therefore, I bless Your Name." The act of worship declares: "I know

You are Jehovah, the Self-Existing One Who is Present to Act in the midst of my situation, so I will stand still and see Your salvation. Your Word says that if I commit the course of my life to You, You will act covereignly to bring Your plan for my life to fruition. So I give You free reign to do what is necessary in my life, because I know that You Are Present to Act so as to accomplish the good work You have begun in me. Therefore, I bless Your Name."

"Worship" is a verb. And, yes, as with most things, action speaks louder than words. "To worship" requires action.

Returning to our text (Psalms100:4), then, we have these three concepts: [1] the **thankful heart** (approaching the Lord "with thanksgiving" and "with praise"), [2] **praise** ("give thanks unto Him") and [3] **worship** ("bless His Name").

Now, having established these concepts and working definitions, we return to the series of commands that have often been viewed as a segmented path from thanksgiving to worship, by way of praise.

[1] Enter into His gates with thanksgiving and into His courts with praise
[2] Be thankful [Give thanks] unto Him, and
[3] Bless His Name.

In the life of the Believer, the thankful heart, praise, and worship should coexist in perfect equilibrium: a triple-point. The three should seamlessly flow into one another. In proper balance, none is more important than any other. None predominates over any other. None has a beginning or ending with respect to any other.

Remember:

[1] The thankful heart is a "thing" – an adjective combined with a noun;
[2] Praise is a voluntary act that gives voice and/or action to the thankfulness in the heart – a verb; and
[3] Worship is the grateful, voluntary surrender of "self" (i.e., will, intellect and emotions) to God – a verb.

I think digression into physical science will help bring the matter to conclusion. . . .

I remember from my days in high school chemistry that there is a point for any pure substance where the three phases of matter – solid, liquid and gas – coexist in perfect equilibrium. It is called the "triple-point." Similarly, there is a point where a thankful heart, praise, and worship coexist in perfect equilibrium: one flowing into the other, seamlessly. The thankfulness in one's heart flows into an act of praise and/or worship, which flows into an act of worship and/or praise, which flows into the thankful heart, which flows into an act of worship and/or praise, which flows into and act of praise and/or worship, etc. Thankfulness is a condition of the heart; praise is an audible and/or visible manifestation of the thankful heart; worship is an act of grateful, personal surrender to God.

When we talk about "praise & worship," as that phrase is bandied about in the Christian lexicon, we are talking about a spiritual place where the conditions are such that we flow – individually and/or corporately – among **thankfulness**, **praise**, and **worship**: thanksgiving erupting into praise; worship reminding us to give thanks and putting thanksgiving in our hearts; praise leading us to value God more and, thus, to worship Him; worship slipping into acts of praise; praise reminding us to be thankful and putting thanksgiving in our hearts, etc.

If you want to know about the "triple-point", ask Shadrach, Meshach and Abednego. You remember the three Hebrew boys who had **thankful hearts** because God had blessed them to prosper in Babylon? They refused to bow down when the king's music was played. Their testimony, in refusing to bow, was a **praise**. Their disregard for personal safety was **worship**. And when their praise flowed into their worship and the thankfulness in their hearts gave birth to their acts praise and their worship. . . . They must have been at the "triple-point" just about the time Nebuchadnezzar had the furnace heated up seven times its normal temperature and had the boys thrown in. God stepped in at the "triple-point" and walked with them in the midst of the furnace, delivering them from the plan of the enemy. And when they came out of the furnace, their enemy, King Nebuchadnezzar, promoted them. (Daniel 3)

Ask **Paul and Silas** about the "triple-point." They were on their way to give thanks to God at the temple in Thyratira (**thankful hearts**) when a member of the Psychic Friends Network started following them and disturbing them. After a few days, Paul got tired of her foolishness and cast out the fortune-telling demon. Knowing that he had no power to get rid of the psychic, himself, Paul called on the Name of Jesus. (That's **worship**.) So he and his buddy got thrown in jail. But the THANKFULNESS in their HEARTS came bubbling out of their mouths around midnight. They began singing and praising God in the deepest, darkest part of the prison. (That's **praise**.) And God sent an earthquake that not only freed Paul and Silas, but freed those around them. (Acts 16)

(When God intervenes at a "triple-point" He may bless you and, in the process, bless those around you. Even the jailor who put Paul and Silas in the stocks in the innermost part of the prison and who was on the verge of committing suicide when he discovered that the gates were open, came to know Jesus, because of Paul and Silas's "triple-point" experience.)

A **thankful heart**, **praise**, and **worship** . . . when these come together in our lives, we allow God to move sovereignly. The result is victory and deliverance. Your breakthrough is at the "triple-point." Your healing is at the "triple-point." Your deliverance is at the "triple-point." And, don't be surprised, if God decides to bless others through you, when your thankful heart and acts of praise and commitment to worship, come together for the glory of God.

As the songwriter says, "With my hands lifted up and my mouth filled with praise, with a heart of thanksgiving I will bless Thee, oh Lord." At my triple-point, I will stand still and see your salvation; I will walk with You in the midst of my fiery furnace; I will witness my deliverance; I will watch you bless me and those around me because of Your sovereign move.

I will **approach You with a thankful heart – a heart full of thanks giving and praise.**

I will **give thanks to You – giving You audible and/visible praise.**

I will **bless Your Name – worshiping You through the grateful, voluntary surrender of "self."**

VII. Sheet Music

"Praise"

"You Are God"

"A Song of Thanks"

"Why My Praise"

"Lord, You Are Great"

Praise

Rodney Teal

A Song of Thanks
(Thank You Lord For All You've Done For Me)

Rodney Teal

You Are God

Rodney Teal

Additional Lyrics:

You are holy.
We adore You.
Lord, we love You.
Lord, You're worthy.
Great Jehovah.
Hallelujah

2002

Why My Praise

3. El Shaddai   4. El Elyon   5. Elohim   6. Holy One   7. Jesus Christ

Lord, You Are Great
(We Praise Your Name)

Rodney Teal

5-9-04

About the Author

Rodney A. Teal is an anointed, multi-gifted member of the Body of Christ and has been intimately involved in ministry as a choir director, preacher, songwriter, praise & worship leader, and teacher for more than 20 years. Presently, he is the Minister of Music at the Israel Baptist Church of Washington, D.C., where Rev. Dr. Morris L. Shearin is Pastor. Rodney served from 1999 – 2006 as the Minister of Music of the Mt. Pleasant Baptist Church in Alexandria, Virginia, where (in December of 2000) he was ordained as Minister of Music and where (in September 2003) he was formally licensed to preach the Gospel.

Rev. Teal has studied piano and voice. He reads music, plays "by ear" and is versed in several sacred music styles, including hymns, anthems, spirituals, traditional gospel, and contemporary gospel. His songwriter's portfolio covers the full range of African-American sacred music. Beyond the technical aspects of music theory and performance, Rev. Teal's ministry focuses on proclaiming the Word of God, particularly as it relates to praise & worship and to ministers of music: singers, songwriters, directors, and musicians.

Rodney's passion is preaching, whether from the pulpit or choir loft. Answering God's call on his life, he has been privileged to serve in music and preaching ministry at churches in Virginia and in the Charleston, West Virginia metropolitan area. He is an active member of the Gospel Music Workshop of America, serving in local and national office and as a faculty member. He is frequently called upon to minister through music and through the preached Word at workshops, conferences, and seminars across the United States.

Minister Teal has earned a Bachelor of Science (Civil Engineering) from VPI&SU (Virginia Tech), a Master of Business Administration from Radford University, a Juris Doctor from Washington & Lee University, and a Master of Divinity from the Howard University School of Divinity.

Rodney is a licensed attorney and is employed as a federal court administrator. He and his wife, Monica, have four children: Elizabeth, James, Ann Marie and Michael. They reside in Alexandria, Virginia.